I0489807

Young Money: A Beginner's Investment Playbook

SPENCER YASAR

Copyright © 2024 Spencer Yasar

All rights reserved.

ISBN: 9798386823603

CONTENTS

1 INTRODUCTION

Introduction

Learning about the stock market and investing is crucial for young investors who want to grow their money, become financially independent, and ultimately plan for their futures. The stock market is a powerful tool that allows investors to grow their money over time and achieve financial goals. While this is true, the stock market is rather complex and comes with both risks and rewards. This novel will go over the importance of having knowledge of the stock market, the basics of investing, basic ways to grow money, and the risks and rewards of the stock market.

Why learning about the stock market is important

Knowledge of the stock market is the most crucial skill for investors to have. Knowledge of the stock market provides investors with ways to grow their wealth and invest. Essentially, investing in the stock market allows investors to participate in the growth of companies or the economy as a whole. By investing your money in the stock market, you are purchasing a small portion of the company. Additionally, the stock market provides a way to diversify one's portfolio and manage their risk.

More importantly, investing in the stock market is a way to achieve long-term financial goals like retirement. By investing in the stock market, investors can take advantage of compound interest over time to grow their money significantly. On the other hand, investors who do not invest in the stock market may struggle to be financially stable due to an inflationary economy.

Another reason why learning about the stock market is crucial is that it provides individuals with general financial literacy. Knowledge of the stock market leads to a general understanding of the economy, managing money, and financial markets. By learning about investing, you can avoid costly mistakes and even achieve financial independence.

The basics of investing and how it works

In simple terms, investing is the process of putting money into an asset, hoping to gain a return. Almost always, investing involves risk because there is no guarantee that a positive return will be earned. While this is true, investing does allow for higher returns than a simple bank savings account, and it can be done with little to no risk.

The most common way to invest is through stocks. Stocks allow for small ownership in a company. When an investor buys a stock, that investor is technically a shareholder in that company. In many cases, the investor even has the right to vote on company decisions. The overall value of the stock is determined by the performance of the company, but also by the performance of the market. Oftentimes, it is hard for a company to allow for positive returns for investors when the market is not performing well. When a company does, then that company would be considered to be "out-performing" the market.

Another way to invest is through bonds. Bonds are debt securities that pay a fixed interest rate. Generally, bonds are considered to have less risk than stocks because they provide a fixed income stream and have a lower chance of losing money. Stocks do not have a fixed income stream and can take an extreme redirection at any given moment, whereas bonds cannot. The caveat here is that bonds offer lower returns than stocks in the long term.

While it may not be as relevant to young investors, investing in real estate is also a popular form of investing. Real estate can provide rental income and capital appreciation over time. Since real estate does require a significant amount of capital and high transaction costs, it is rather risky.

Last but not least are mutual funds. Partaking in mutual funds and exchange-traded funds (ETFs) allows individuals a way to invest in a diversified portfolio of stocks and bonds without directly managing them themselves. These funds are professionally managed and offer investors exposure to many companies and even industries. There are many types of mutual funds that entail a wide variety of risk and reward goals that will be discussed later in this book.

The risks and rewards of investing in the stock market

Being an investor in the stock market can allow for significant rewards, but it also comes with risks that should be carefully considered. One of the main risks of investing in the stock market is the chance of simply losing money. Values of stocks vary significantly depending on the day, based on both the overall economy's performance and the

individual company's performance. If an investor purchases a stock and the company performs poorly, the stock will depreciate in value, causing a potential risk for the investor.

An additional risk of investing in the stock market is market volatility. The stock market often experiences sharp declines in value in response to economic conditions. These conditions may be inflation or even a recession. The potential volatility may be unsettling for investors, which may cause them to make poor decisions with their money in panic. A smart investor will logically think through these situations and make decisions that make sense for the long term.

In addition to these risks, investing requires knowledge and skill. Not knowing what you are doing is a risk in itself. Investors must be able to analyze the performance and make skilled decisions regarding their portfolios. If the investor lacks the knowledge and skill, then they may make poor decisions. With that said, part of gaining the skill and knowledge is by learning in action, so investing a small amount of money to learn what you need to do is never a bad idea.

While there are many risks, the stock market offers many rewards, which is why it is so appealing to investors. The main reward of the stock market is the potential to receive high returns. Looking at past years, the stock market generates an average return of about 8-10%. These returns are what allow investors to grow their wealth and achieve their financial aspirations.

Another reward of investing is the ability to earn money through dividends. Dividends are distributions of profits to shareholders. Dividends are essentially extra money gained in addition to the value of the stock. Many companies pay dividends to their shareholders, which can provide another income stream that may be steadier than just managing stocks.

The stock market also offers diversification benefits. By investing in a variety of stocks, investors reduce their overall risk and achieve higher returns. Investing in the stock market also allows for exposure to different industries and regions of the world. Many investors invest in industries that they would not otherwise be familiar with, as well as regions of the world that they may not have otherwise been involved in. Investing in these different regions of the world allows investors to be a part of the global economy.

Investing in the stock market allows for significant rewards but also comes with risks that must be considered. Investors should always be prepared to lose money and have a beyond solid understanding of every company that they are investing in. With all these things considered and keeping a long-term investment strategy, investing in the stock market is one of the most powerful ways to grow money and achieve your financial goals.

2 THE STOCK MARKET: BASICS

What the stock market is and how it operates

The stock market is an economic platform where both buyers and sellers trade holdings or shares of publicly traded companies. It allows businesses to raise capital by selling holdings to the public. Then, your everyday investors can buy and sell shares to make a return on their capital. If you have ever watched Shark Tank, the process is very similar. You are investing in a company based on whether you think the company is going to perform well. Then, your money appreciates as the company grows and depreciates if the company performs poorly. The only main difference is that your common investor invests on a much smaller scale. The stock market's main operating feature is supply and demand. The price of any given stock is determined by the number of buyers and sellers in the market; this is how the price of a stock changes so rapidly.

When a company decides to go public and sell shares of the company to the public, it is most often executed through an IPO, or an Initial Public Offering. During an IPO, the company determines a fixed number of shares to offer to the public at a predetermined price. After this, the shares are then traded on the stock market. It is very difficult to get shares of a company in its initial public offering. Shares are often distributed to very high-net-worth clients. Regardless, once these shares are on the stock market, the price fluctuates just like any other stock based on financial performance, industry trends, and the market conditions that pertain to all stocks.

The stock market is divided into two main categories: primary and secondary markets. The primary market consists of companies issuing new shares of stock to raise capital. On the other hand, the secondary market consists of investors buying and selling existing shares of stock. There are many secondary markets. The most well-known are the New York Stock Exchange, or the NYSE, the NASDAQ, or even the Chicago Stock Exchange. These secondary markets put together composites, which are essentially performance averages of all their companies, that investors can view to get a consensus of market performance.

Oftentimes, when small investors intend to buy or sell shares of stock, they use a brokerage firm. Brokerage firms are essentially mediators between buyers and sellers who execute trades on behalf of their clients. Brokerage firms make money by charging fees that include general fees for holding an account or commission on trades made.

The stock market is also subject to regulation by the government, specifically the Securities and Exchange Commission (SEC). The SEC is responsible for enforcing the many laws that relate to trading on the stock market and regulating the accuracy of the information given to investors from each company. Every person who has money in a company is an investor and deserves accurate information on the market, which is why the SEC is crucial. The SEC is also the main regulator of insider trading. Insider trading is the illegal practice of trading based on non-public information. For example, if I knew someone who worked for Meta's corporate office and learned through them that Meta was releasing a new social media platform, and because of that information, I bought shares, that would be insider trading because I traded based on non-public or insider information.

As assumed, investing in the stock market comes with its risks simply because the market is volatile and can change rather suddenly. While this is true, it is one of the most lucrative ways to build wealth over time, especially if you are diligent and create a diversified portfolio.

In conclusion, the stock market is a vital feature of our economy that allows companies to raise capital and grow their businesses, in addition to investors having the opportunity to make a profit by buying and selling shares of stock. While the stock market is complex, it is one of the best methods for capital growth and financial stability.

3 THE STOCK MARKET: KEY TERMS

Key terms and concepts

Anyone who has been in an investing environment knows that there are numerous terms and concepts that you must know to understand and communicate about the market. Here are some of the most important terms and concepts.

1. Stock - A stock, also known as a share or even equity, is a part of ownership in a company. Buying a stock allows you to be a shareholder and have a claim on your portion of a company's assets and earnings.

2. Market capitalization - Market capitalization, most commonly referred to as a market cap, is the total value of a company's current purchased shares of stock. It is a simple equation calculated by multiplying the

company's stock price by the number of purchased shares.

3. Dividend - Dividends are payments made by a company to its shareholders, most often out of its profits. Dividends are paid either in the form of additional shares or simply with cash. Dividends are up to a company to distribute and are a compelling factor for investors.

4. Price-to-earnings ratio - The price-to-earnings(P/E) ratio is a valuation ratio that

    compares a company's stock price to its earnings per share (EPS). Higher P/E ratios show that stocks are overvalued, and lower P/E ratios show that a stock is undervalued. This ratio is a clear way to determine if you want to invest in a company, with the thought in mind that these ratios can be extremely volatile.

5. Volatility - Volatility is how much a stock price fluctuates or changes over time. The higher the volatility of a stock is, the riskier it is, and vice versa.

6. Index - An index or composite is a group of stocks that represent the overall performance of an entire market or a specific sector. The S&P 500 and the Dow Jones Industrial Average are great examples of indices.

7. Bull Market - A bull market is a time when stock prices are rising, investors are generally

positive, and there is a high overall return on investment (ROI). Investors will often say a company is "Bullish".

8. Bear Market - A bear market is a time when stock prices are decreasing, investors are somewhat negative, and there is not a high ROI. Investors will often say a company is "Bearish".

9. Diversification - Diversification is the practice of distributing your capital across a wide variety of stocks, sectors, or even regions. The main objective of diversification is to reduce risk and optimize return.

10. Risk tolerance - Risk tolerance refers to the amount of willingness an investor has to take on risk to achieve financial goals. Risk tolerance varies based on the objective of the investments and overall financial situation.

While some of these terms may be self-explanatory, they are crucial to understanding the stock market. Familiarizing yourself with these concepts allows you to make informed decisions about investments and navigate the market with confidence.

Different types of stocks and how they differ

There are several kinds of stocks available to investors, each having its characteristics and risks.

Here are some of the most common types of stocks and how they differ:

1. Common Stock - Common stock is the most basic type of holding. It represents a simple share in a company. Holders of the common stock can vote on company decisions and receive dividends, but are last to receive payments if a company goes bankrupt or gets liquidated.

2. Preferred Stock - A preferred stock pays a fixed dividend and has priority over the common stock in the event of bankruptcy or liquidation. While this is true, preferred stockholders often do not have voting rights.

3. Blue-Chip Stocks - Blue-chip stocks are large, established companies that are historically stable and have consistent earnings. They are generally lower risk and lower return, but are reliable for long-term capital growth. Examples of blue-chip stocks are Walmart, Amazon, and Google.

4. Growth Stocks - Growth stocks are stocks in companies that are expected to outperform the entirety of the market and grow at a rather fast rate. These stocks often have high P/E ratios and no dividends, but have the potential for higher earnings. Tesla is a good example of a growth stock, with the thought that growth stocks are not always growth stocks.

5. Value stocks - Value stocks are stocks that are considered to be undervalued by the market. These stocks have low P/E ratios, pay dividends, and may be riskier. Citicorp is often referred to as a value stock.
6. Small-cap Stocks - Small-cap stocks are stocks with relatively low market caps. These stocks have a high potential for growth compared to established companies, but may be riskier.
7. Mid-cap stocks - Mid-cap stocks are stocks with market caps in between small and large-cap stocks. They have a balance of risk and growth. In my opinion, they are the ultimate sweet spot, and having the majority of your holdings in this category is a good idea.
8. Large-cap stocks - Large-cap stocks are stocks with a market cap of $10 billion or more. These are often blue-chip stocks with a low risk and lower growth. They are fundamental and, in my opinion, should be a part of everyone's portfolio.
9. Penny stocks - Penny stocks are stocks with a low stock price. They often trade for less than $5 a share. They are often high-risk and can be fraudulent.

Having a general understanding of the types of stocks is very important for investing and communication. With consideration of the pros and cons of every type of stock, investors can build the ultimate diversified portfolio that is personalized to their needs.

4 CONDUCTING RESEARCH

How to research and analyze stocks

As easy as investing can appear, it does require research and analysis to make informed decisions. First, it is beneficial to determine your financial goals and risk tolerance. Doing so will help you choose the types of stocks that fit your personal situation. For example, if your goal is to make quicker money, it may make sense to invest in more volatile stocks with a higher risk. Otherwise, if you are looking for more stable investments for the long run, then you may consider blue-chip and large-cap stocks that are more stable and have historical evidence of a positive ROI. Once you understand your investment goals and risk tolerance, you must identify the specific stocks you would want to put your money into. I recommend using any resources online, including financial news websites, stock screening tools, and investment newsletters. Doing this will help find stocks that fit your investment criteria, like size, sector, and financial performance. Remember to make sure you check multiple sources; if multiple sources are saying that a stock has growth potential, it is more likely to be true.

Another thing to consider when deciding which stocks to invest in is current events. Current events have a significant impact on the entire stock market, but factors that affect the entire market may not help you find the specific stocks you would like to invest in. Instead, view current events by sector. If there is an increased specific need for a sector, then you can assume that the stock will increase. For example, if there is a war going on in the world, you can assume that the defense sector will grow because of the need. An example occurring in 2023 is within the artificial intelligence and microchip sectors. Because of the increased use of artificial intelligence, many AI stocks rapidly increased, in addition to the microchip stocks that power artificial intelligence.

Another important thing to consider when analyzing stocks is to view the company's management team and corporate structure. A strong management team that is historically reliable can assist in long-term growth and success. On the other hand, a weak management team can lead to poor financial performance and, subsequently, a decline in stock price. A company's board of directors can also be considered to determine if the members provide insight to grow the company.

Finally, based on your research, you can determine the fair value of the stock. You can do so through various valuation metrics such as the P/E ratio. By using a metric to determine if a stock is undervalued or overvalued, you can make an educated decision about whether the stock is worth the risk, capital, or time.

The research element of choosing stocks should not be overlooked, as it is crucial to being an intelligent investor and growing capital. Through this process, you can make proper investment decisions that help you achieve your financial goals.

Fundamental analysis vs. technical analysis

As you learn about investing, you may come across two methods of analyzing stocks: fundamental and technical analysis. Having an understanding of the differences between the approaches can help you make informed decisions.

Fundamental analysis is the process of examining a company's financial statements and other qualitative and quantitative factors in order to determine its value. Factors that are looked at include revenue, earnings, assets, liabilities, cash flow, market share, management, competitive position, and even growth prospects. Fundamental analysis is practiced with the goal of identifying stocks that are undervalued or overvalued by looking at the company's true metrics.

On the other hand, technical analysis examines past market data, like price or volume, with the goal of identifying trends and patterns used to predict the future market. Technical analysis includes charts and technical indicators like moving averages, support and resistance levels, and relative strength. This assists in identifying buy and sell signals. The goal of this is to identify opportunities to profit from these price movements.

While both techniques are commonly used, they both have significant pros and cons. Fundamental analysis is used as a long-term approach simply because it looks at the fundamentals of the company and whether it has the potential to grow steadily. This approach is great for individuals hoping to grow capital over time, build a diversified portfolio, or save for retirement and long-term goals.

Technical analysis is a more short-term approach since it focuses on trends and patterns for quick trading. Technical analysis is perfect for investors who intend to take advantage of short-term price movements. While all of this is true, the market does not always follow patterns and trends. The market is highly volatile, and patterns do not always help indicate the future.

Neither of these approaches is foolproof. Both have limitations and advantages. Fundamental analysis is weak in resisting unforeseen events, either in the general economy, a sector, or just the company in question. Technical analysis is weak in resisting sudden changes in the market sentiment, which are unpredictable.

All types of financial analysis are subjective, and the "best approach" is subject to the investor and their goals. Some may find that a combination of the two is best, while others will find one that works for them. Regardless of the approach, it is important to be analytical and conduct research before making decisions. Always consider the potential risks and rewards of an investment opportunity; more often than not, it is too good to be true.

Using financial statements and ratios to evaluate a company

Now that the basics have been established on types of analysis, we can go deeper into evaluating a specific company's financial statements and ratios, which is an important part of evaluating a company.

A company's financial statements are a perfect overview of its financial stability and performance over a given period of time. There are three main types of financial statements: the income statement, balance sheet, and cash flow statement. The income statement indicated revenue, expenses, and profits or losses. The balance sheet indicates assets, liabilities, and equity at a specific point in time. The cash flow statement indicates the cash inflows and outflows of a company.

Once you understand these financial statements, you can use financial ratios to evaluate their performance. Here are a few ratios you can use:

- Price-to-earnings (P/E) ratio - This ratio measures the price of the company's stock relative to its earnings per share.
- Debt-to-equity (D/E) ratio - This measures a company's debt in relation to its equity. This ratio can reveal if a company is highly leveraged, which can increase risk.
- Return on equity (ROE) - This measures a company's net income relative to its shareholder equity. A high ROE indicates that a company has enough current assets to cover its short-term liabilities.

- Current ratio - This simply measures whether a company is able to pay its short-term debts. The higher the ratio, the higher the ability of the company.

- Gross margin - This measures a company's gross profit in relation to its revenue. A high ratio means that the company is generating significant profits.

Examining a company's financial statements and ratios provides insight into the company's financial health and performance, helping them make informed investment decisions. It is important to note that these ratios are not a clear method of understanding a company's financials. An intelligent move would be to use these ratios with other research and analysis to determine if the investment is worth your money. It is always important to conduct thorough research and analysis before making decisions.

5 DIVERSIFICATION

Diversification and why it matters

Diversification is an optimal strategy for investors. For context, diversification is the practice of investing in a variety of stocks, sectors, and asset classes, rather than solely investing in one single stock or sector. By diversifying their investments, investors can reduce risk and increase returns potential.

The main objective of diversification is that it helps to mitigate the risks of investing in the stock market. Each stock has its own risks, like industry disruptions, economic downturns, and changes in consumer behavior. Investing in a variety of stocks helps reduce exposure to these risks, and their portfolio does not depend on one single stock or industry. For example, if all of your money is in

Target and Target's sales start to decline, your entire portfolio will be declining. If you have 20% in the retail industry like Target, 20% in technology, etc, then you will not be largely affected by the downfall of a specific industry or company.

Another clear benefit of diversifying your portfolio is that it can help stabilize your portfolio through the ups and downs of the market. Asset classes tend to perform differently depending on market conditions. By distributing your capital in different asset classes, you can avoid the volatility of your portfolio and gain stable returns.

Additionally, diversifying your portfolio can help you be resilient to a recession. A recession is a period of time when the economy declines along with trade and industrial activity. Oftentimes, throughout recessions, certain industries outperform the market and prove to be resilient against the economic decline. By diversifying your portfolio, you have a much higher chance of being resilient because you will have holdings in multiple industries.

Like all other methods, diversification does not guarantee profits or protect against losses. While this is true, it does help reduce overall risk and increase returns over the long term if it is done properly. Proper diversification includes a variety of stocks and asset classes like large-cap and small-cap stocks, growth and value stocks, domestic and international stocks, and bonds and commodities.

A way for investors to achieve diversification is through mutual funds and ETFs. These methods allow for exposure to a variety of stocks and asset classes with a single investment. For instance, an index fund for the S&P 500 would provide exposure to many large-cap stocks, allowing you to have holdings in many companies without investing in each individually, ultimately leading to a more diversified portfolio.

The only exception to the rule of always diversifying your portfolio is if you are investing with high risk and want to put all of your money into one industry. This is the easiest way to make a lot of money, but it is also the easiest way to lose all of your money. More often than not, you lose your money. Diversifying your portfolio avoids losing your money, but if this is a strategy that you would like to take, you don't always have to diversify your portfolio.

To conclude, diversification is a crucial strategy for investing. It allows for mitigating risk, having a resilient portfolio, and having holdings in different industries. It can allow for higher returns and is ultimately one of the fundamentals of investing.

6 INVESTING STRATEGIES

Different investment strategies and approaches

Using previously discussed terminology relating to stock types, we can now establish investing strategies. There are many strategies that investors can consider. Each has its benefits and drawbacks, and the right strategy is dependent on investment goals, risk tolerance, and financial situation.

1. Value investing - Value investing is the practice of buying stocks that are undervalued, with the expectation that they will rise to their true value.
2. Growth investing - Growth investing is the practice of buying stocks with high growth potential, regardless of the stock price.
3. Income investing - Income investing is the practice of buying stocks that pay high dividends, hoping to create steady income from the dividends.

4. Index investing - Index investing is the practice of buying a portfolio of stocks that follows a market index like the S&P 500.
5. Contrarian - Contrarian investing is the practice of buying stocks that are out of favor with the market, hoping that the stocks will rebound.
6. Momentum Investing - Momentum investing is the practice of buying stocks that have recently performed well, hoping that they will continue to rise.
7. Dollar-cost averaging - Dollar-cost averaging involves investing a fixed amount of money into a stock or fund regardless of the stock price.

Long-term vs short-term investing

When investing, you can follow either a long-term or short-term investment strategy. While it is true for all strategies, for this one especially, your approach depends on your goals. If you are investing for retirement, then you should adopt a long-term approach, but if you are investing for quick money, then adopt a short-term approach. It is entirely situational.

Long-term investing entails holding on to stocks for an extended period of time, oftentimes years or decades. The goal of this investing type is to generate higher returns over the long term, instead of short-term gains. The main element of long-term investing is buying a share and holding onto it regardless of short-term market fluctuations. If a stock goes down 5%, it is less important with this approach because the stock will most likely rebound before it intends to sell. This method is low maintenance because there is no need to watch the market very closely. You should still be in the loop, but there is no need to check in daily or even weekly.

Long-term investments typically generate strong returns over time. The market grows in the long term, so holding on to stocks for multiple years or decades allows for your capital to grow with the market. Compound interest is also significant because the returns earned are reinvested and can generate higher returns. On average, capital held in the stock market grows about 10% per year. While it may seem low, it adds up over time.

Short-term investing entails purchasing and selling stocks over a short period of time; on average, that time period is about a few months. Short-term investors are able to take advantage of short-term market changes and can generate quick profits. Additionally, short-term investors can take advantage of current market trends that may not last decades. Short-term investing is often risky because of the difficulty in predicting market movements, especially short-term movements. Short-term investing is for investors with a high level of knowledge and skill and who are willing to take on risks; it is a more advanced approach to investing.

For newer investors, especially younger ones, long-term investing is the safest bet, but attempting short-term investing with small amounts of money with the goal of learning the market is not a bad approach either. By adopting a buy-and-hold strategy, investors take advantage of the longevity of the market and do not have to watch the market closely.

Both methods have advantages and disadvantages, but both are viable options that can grow your capital. While long-term investing is the safest bet, if you are diligent and do your research, there is no problem with short-term investing. If you devote your time to investing, short-term investing might even be fit for your situation. To conclude, by looking at their situation, investors can make the correct choice for their portfolio, whether they want quick cash or long-term gains.

Value investing vs. growth investing

Value investing and growth investing are two of the most popular investment strategies in the stock market. Both methods require evaluation and research, but are great for creating an intelligent portfolio. Many new and young investors may be interested in these strategies as they are both simple and effective.

Value investing entails purchasing stocks that are undervalued by the market. Investors then expect the stock to rise to its appropriate value. Value investors tend to focus on companies that have strong fundamentals like low price-to-earnings ratios, high dividends, and a good history of earnings. The goal of value investing is to be ahead of the market in recognizing the true value of the company itself.

Growth investing entails purchasing stocks from companies that have strong growth potential. Growth investors do not focus on stock price and tend not to care if the stock price is high compared to its earnings. Growth investors purchase stock in companies that are expected to grow faster than the market and can deliver returns over the long term. Growth companies often fundamentally focus on expansion and growing their business, which can lead to strong growth. An example of an expanding growth stock is Apple. Apple started in the computer industry, then expanded into the mobile device industry, then the watch industry, and then the banking industry. Their constant focus on growth is what is appealing to investors who take a growth investing approach.

A benefit of value investing is that it helps to mitigate risk. The undervalued stocks that are purchased with value investing have a safety margin and are not likely to experience sharp declines in value. Value stocks are often less volatile than growth stocks, which can create stability in a portfolio.

Growth investing has its benefits as well. Growth investing can generate higher returns over the long term since the growth stocks are projected to grow fast and strong. Growth stocks may also have a higher valuation relative to their earnings, but if the company grows at the expected rate, the valuation may become more reasonable over time.

Both value and growth investing have their risks and potential rewards, and like other strategies, are situational. Value investing is typically the choice for investors who are looking for stability, while growth investing may be better for investors who are looking for more risk. Both are viable options that can have significant upside for investors.

Dollar-cost averaging and other investment techniques

Now that the basic strategies have been covered, there are more advanced strategies that are used by many investors. All are great for generating upside, but have distinct differences.

One popular method is dollar-cost averaging. Dollar-cost averaging entails investing a fixed amount of money into a stock or fund at regular intervals, regardless of the stock price. Oftentimes, investors will invest a small amount of money at a time. Investing a small, fixed amount of money allows for reducing the impact of market volatility on investment returns. Dollar-cost averaging is somewhat niche and is not used by the everyday investor, but when it is, it has the potential for significant upside.

Rebalancing is another technique that investors can consider. Rebalancing entails periodically adjusting the allocation of assets in a portfolio to maintain a target mix of investments based on market conditions. For instance, if your portfolio is 60% stocks and 40% bonds and the stock market is performing well, you may rebalance to a portfolio that is 70% stocks and 30% bonds. This is done by selling some of their bonds and using that capital for the stock market, and vice versa.

Tax-loss harvesting is another investment strategy to consider. Tax-loss harvesting entails selling losing investments to offset gains from other investments and reduce tax liability. If an investor has a stock that has lost value, they may sell it at a loss to offset the gains from a stock that has increased in value. This helps to reduce an investor's overall tax liability and increase net returns.

A general strategy for investing is to consider the taxes and fees that may affect your return. Potential fees include trading fees, expense ratios, and account fees. These fees can easily impact the overall returns of your portfolio. It is crucial to review the fees that are associated with investment products and look for low-cost options that can aid in maximizing returns.

In summary, there are many investment techniques and strategies available to investors to consider when investing. By carefully selecting what is relevant to their portfolio, investors can reach their financial goals and grow their investing skills along with their capital.

7 RISK MANAGEMENT

Understanding risk and volatility

As you venture into the stock market, it is crucial to understand what risk and volatility are conceptually. Risk is the potential of losing money or capital on an investment. On the other hand, volatility is the degree of fluctuation of a stock. Both of these factors are inherently significant in investing and must be considered when making an investment.

As simple as it seems, the key risk in investing is losing money. As previously mentioned, stocks are affected by an abundance of factors like economic conditions, industry disruptions, and the behaviors of consumers. These factors point to how investors need to weigh the risks when investing. Always ask yourself if each stock is worth the risk.

Volatility is the degree of fluctuation in either a single stock price or the entire market over time. Stocks that are considered to be high-volatility will often experience larger swings in price, while low-volatility stocks are more stable. Volatility is caused by many factors, like general market conditions, company news, and the ever-changing point of view of investors.

Both risk and volatility may be daunting to investors, but they have their positive benefits. Risk and volatility are also opportunities for possible returns. High-risk investments can be associated with higher returns, and low-risk investments can be associated with stable and lower returns. Like risk, high-volatility investments have the potential for high risk in the long term, and low-volatility stocks hold the potential for stable and lower returns.

It is important to conduct thorough research before investing in any stock, in addition to monitoring investments after they have been executed to make sure that the risk or volatility has not increased since execution. The overall understanding of risk and volatility is crucial to creating a balanced portfolio.

How to manage risk in a portfolio

Managing risk is a crucial aspect of investing, especially for those just starting out. Unfortunately, you can never fully get rid of risk, but various strategies can be used to aid the management of risk and reduce the likelihood of losses. The main strategy for managing risk is diversification, but that has already been discussed in depth, so there are a few others that may be helpful for investors.

The first strategy is to set stop-loss orders on investments. This is one of the best ways to automate the management of risk. This strategy is phenomenal for investors who may not have the time to watch the market on a very frequent basis. These orders automatically sell a stock if the price of the stock falls below a certain price. They are very helpful for limiting losses and allow for the risk to be lower because you choose how much money you can potentially lose.

As boring as it is, the other main strategy for risk management is just doing research, analyzing market trends, and practicing thorough analysis to make sure that there is no significant risk in a stock. All of these steps can help you make informed decisions about a stock and potentially limit the risk.

Additionally, it is important to stick to a long-term investment strategy. Risk is low when you invest in companies with longevity that you know will appreciate over time. This will allow you not to take action on short-term market fluctuations and instead focus on long-term goals. Ultimately, staying disciplined is the easiest way to limit risk.

At the moment, investors can also rebalance their portfolios to make sure their portfolio is low risk.

Adjusting your portfolio is the best way to create longevity with your portfolio because you are adapting it to the market's trends. Adjustments allow a portfolio to thrive, grow, and stay low-risk.

Dealing with market downturns and bear markets

When investing in the stock market, market downturns and bear markets are virtually inevitable. Even when you know that this is normal, it can still be unsettling to watch your money depreciate, but most of the time, it is just temporary and will rise back up.

The best thing to do in a situation where the market depreciates is to avoid making irrational and emotional decisions. Selling all of your stocks in panic can be one of the worst decisions you make because, oftentimes, when panicking, you will sell them at a loss and miss out on the future upside of the stock. Alternatively, think of the long term, do your research, and make smart, logical decisions.

One of the best ways to tell if you should sell a stock in a hurry is simply by determining why the stock depreciated. When drawing this conclusion, I recommend looking at one thing: whether the stock depreciated because of something the company did or because of the market and consumers. If the company made a bad decision, then it may be a good idea to sell because that can be an indicator that the company is poorly managed and will not appreciate anytime soon. If consumers are overreacting or the entire market or sector is depreciating, then it might be worth doing more digging to determine if you truly want to sell. A good example of this is Corona Beer's parent company, Constellation Brands. In 2020, this stock almost halved because COVID-19 was also known as the Coronavirus. The consumer market overreacted and made uneducated decisions, and within a year, the stock was higher than the price before it halved. The smart move here was to wait it out because the company did not make any intelligent moves.

It is also important for investors to have realistic expectations about the stock market. Very rarely will the stock market increase at a steady rate. Expect ups and downs, and, as mentioned before, do not make irrational decisions. My best advice is to ride out periods of market volatility to achieve your financial goals.

Finally, take advantage of bear markets. The fundamental of investing is to buy the dip. When a stock is low and has growth potential, buy it so you can benefit. If you are always being harmed by bear markets, then you most likely will not benefit as much as you can. It is inevitable to be harmed by bear markets temporarily, but take advantage of the bear markets too, so you can benefit from them as well.

Risk management is one of the fundamentals of investing. By taking appropriate measures, being diligent, and making informed decisions, investors can optimize their portfolios and have the most upside possible.

8 GETTING STARTED

Setting investment goals and objectives

As obvious as it seems, setting investment goals is very important for investors, especially younger ones. Investing goals promote discipline and ensure that every choice an investor makes is appropriate for their goals.

The very first thing that must be established in setting investment goals is determining what you want to get out of the process of investing and your financial needs. Do you want to learn, or are you trying to make money? Do you have any large financial commitments in the near future, such as college payments or a down payment on a house? How much time do you want to spend on investing, and how much money are you willing to spend? All of these questions will aid in determining your risk tolerance and what you are trying to get out of the investing process.

The next step is to determine the risk level that you are willing to take on. Do you need a quick return? If so, high-risk investments may be your best bet, keeping in mind that you have a higher chance of losses. Or, are you thinking of the long-term? In that case, low-risk stocks are your best bet. Determining your risk level will allow you to set your investing goals.

The final step in determining your goals is establishing your timeline. When creating your timeline, keep in mind the amount of time you need to get your portfolio to where you want it to be, in addition to the level of risk that is appropriate for the goal. You should also periodically review your goals and timeline in order to make adjustments when necessary.

Overall, setting investment goals is crucial to being a successful investor, especially at first. By following all of the previously listed steps, you can identify what you are trying to get out of investing, your risk tolerance, and your timeline to ensure success. Do not forget to adjust your plan as time goes on to fit your goals.

Opening a brokerage account and buying your first stock

Opening a brokerage account is both an exciting and educational process, especially for younger investors.

It is important to note that investors under 18 cannot hold sole ownership of a brokerage account, but with the help of a parent or guardian, you can hold partial rights to a custodial account. Custodial accounts still give you the right to buy and sell stocks, but with a few modifications. Nonetheless, it is still a way to learn and put your money to work.

1. Choose a brokerage firm: There are numerous brokerage firms. Some are larger banks like E*TRADE, which is owned by Morgan Stanley. Others are smaller online brokers like Robinhood. Both are viable options, but the best way to choose is by assessing factors like fees, customer service, investment options, and even educational resources.

2. Open an account: Once you know which brokerage firm you want to trade with, you can open an account either online or in person, depending on the firm. You will need to provide personal information like a Social Security number, income, and employment information.

3. Fund your account: Before you are able to trade, you need funds in the brokerage account to trade with. To do this, you will need to transfer money from your bank account to your brokerage account. Alternatively, you can deposit a check to transfer funds.

4. Research stocks: Previously, we went over the ways you can research a stock. Use those methods, but there are often research tools within the brokerage firm's website that you can use.

5. Place a trade: Once you choose the stock you want to buy, you should then place an order. You will need to enter the stock's ticker symbol, the number of shares you would like to buy, and sometimes the price you are willing to pay.

Having a brokerage account holds a lot of responsibility and a lot of risk. When you have your account, make sure to make informed decisions and distribute your money wisely. For younger investors, you may have the advantage of time. It may be smart to take longer-term approaches and reap the benefits of compounded returns if you have many years ahead. Alternatively, have fun with the account. Make investments that you can watch closely as well. There is no wrong way to invest, but know that you should evaluate risk as much as you can.

Using a brokerage account intelligently

Once you are executing trades and investing your money, there are a few other methods you can take on to optimize potential returns and make the most capital you can. There are also certain habits that investors should have to be a consistent and effective investor.

First, starting small may be a good strategy for beginners. A good method is to start investing with a small amount of money and gradually increase your investment as you learn more about the market and its operations. Never invest more than you can afford to lose, and with less experience comes more risk, so by starting small, investors can gain experience and knowledge about the market with limited risk.

Secondly, you should invest regularly, even if each increment is not a large amount. Doing so can help you build your portfolio over time and also take advantage of market fluctuations. This approach can also help you avoid making impulsive decisions. Finally, regularly investing keeps you informed on the market. It requires you to do more research and stay informed about what is happening in the market.

Another great tip for investing is to seek advice from professionals or experienced investors. Asking people about their investing decisions helps you gain insight into the market and how others invest. This is great for building your strategy and investing habits. If you do not know any investors, then there are many investment clubs or online forums that allow you to connect with other investors. Reading online is the ultimate strategy to gain insight because there is so much knowledge at the click of a button.

By keeping good strategies and habits like investing in increments and starting small, investors can optimize their returns and create a well-thought-out portfolio.

9 BUDGETING

Introduction to budgeting

Budgeting is one of the most important practices, especially when wanting to invest. Budgeting can transform your financial situation, even if you do not have a lot of money to begin with, leaving money to invest.

The first step towards budgeting is to understand income and expenses. Calculate your income, including allowances or any other type of income. Then, make a list of expenses and determine if they are fixed, such as rent or car payments, or variable, like groceries or entertainment. By understanding your inflows and outflows financially, you can evaluate your spending for budgeting.

To stretch your resources, it may be helpful to differentiate between needs and wants. Needs are essential for survival, and wants are to bring pleasure or convenience. When budgeting optimally, prioritize needs and allocate funds accordingly. Keep in mind that spending habits help allocate more money towards saving and investing.

Create a realistic budget

After understanding income and expenses, it may be time to create a realistic budget. Set aside money for fixed expenses, ensuring that there is enough money for these essentials. Then assign a portion of your income to your variable expenses. Try to minimize this category, but remember that it is ok to treat yourself, even on an optimal budget. Then set aside a percentage of your income for saving and investing. Even if only a small amount is left, budgeting can help you leave you with the money you need to start.

Tracking spending is a critical component of budgeting, allowing monitoring of expenses, identifying areas with overspending, and making the necessary adjustments. Reviewing patterns and analyzing them can help cut back without sacrificing needs. By being conscious of spending habits, you can develop a better understanding of your financial situation and make informed decisions.

Budgeting is the foundation of financial success, regardless of income size. By understanding income and expenses, you can begin your journey to gaining

the amount of money you need to invest in the stock
market.

10 TAXES AND ACCOUNTS

The impact of taxes on investments

With the expansive world of investing comes taxes. Taxes are often dreaded, but taxes are an important factor that affects investment returns. In simple terms, taxes are a method for governments to collect revenue and fund public services like infrastructure, education, and healthcare. Taxes can also eat into investment returns, especially if you do not know how taxes affect your investments.

Many different types of taxes can impact investment returns. The most common type is capital gains tax. This is simply a tax on the profits made from selling an investment. If you buy a stock for $100 and sell it for $150, the profit is $50. Depending on the tax laws, capital gains tax will likely have to be paid, and the tax rate can vary depending on how long it was held, income level, and type of investment. In the USA, the rates are 0%, 15%, or 20%, depending on your taxable income and filing status. The important aspect to remember about capital gains tax is that it is levied on the profits.

An additional type of tax that can impact investment returns is dividend tax. This is made on the dividends you receive from a company you have invested in. Depending on tax laws, investors may have to pay taxes on the dividends received. For dividend tax, the respective dividends must be

"qualified," meaning that they meet special requirements issued by the IRS to be taxed at capital gains tax rates.

Taxes have a significantly large impact on investments and investment returns over the long term. If you invest $1,000 in a stock that grows at an average rate of 7% per year, the investment will be worth $7,612 after 30 years. However, if capital gains taxes need to be paid, the 20% tax required upon the sale of the stock will cause the stock to only be worth $6,089 after 30 years. This is an example of how significant the difference in returns is with and without taxes.

The awareness of tax implications is especially important in planning. One strategy for minimizing the impact of taxes on investment returns is to minimize the tax impact, such as with tax-exempt bonds or tax-deferred investment accounts. These are investments specifically structured to minimize tax impact.

Another strategy is to hold on to investments for the long term. If you hold an investment for more than a year, you may be eligible for a lower tax rate on capital gains. This is known as the long-term capital gains rate and can be lower than the short-term capital gains rate. The differentiation poses one of the downfalls of short-term investing.

Taxes can have a significant impact on investment returns, but there are strategies that can be used to reduce the impact. By being aware of the tax implications of investments, returns can be maximized.

Different types of accounts and their tax implications

When investing, there are many types of accounts that can be considered, especially for beginners. Each type of account has its own tax implications, which can affect how much money investors take home.

The first type of account that can be considered is a traditional individual retirement account (IRA). With a traditional IRA, individuals contribute pre-tax dollars, meaning they can deduct their contributions from their taxable income for the year. This can result in a lower tax bill for the year when the contributions are made. However, when the investor withdraws funds from the account, they will owe taxes on those funds at the ordinary tax rate.

Another option is the Roth IRA. With this account, investors contribute after-tax dollars, meaning they cannot deduct their contributions from their taxable income for the year. However, when the investors withdraw funds from the retirement account, they will not owe any taxes on the funds, as they have already paid back taxes. This means that the gains will not be taxed, creating a significantly low tax rate overall. This account is especially useful for teenagers, as a teenager's tax bracket will most likely increase between their current age and retirement. There are also income limits on the Roth IRA, so once an investor makes a certain amount of money, their Roth IRA can no longer be added to.

A third option is a taxable brokerage account. With this account, investors contribute after-tax dollars and do not receive tax benefits for contributions, but they also do not owe taxes on their contributions or gains in the account until they sell an asset and realize a gain. At this point, they will owe taxes on the gain, but only at the capital gains tax rate, which is often lower than the ordinary income tax rate.

In addition to these accounts, young investors may also consider custodial accounts, which are accounts that adults set up for minors. The adult serves as the custodian of the account until the minor reaches a certain age, at which point they become the owner of the account. Custodial accounts can be opened as virtually any type of account and have the same tax benefits as the corresponding type of account. A custodial account does not reap any special benefits, but simply is a way for young investors to begin investing.

Tax-efficient investing strategies

With the various types of accounts to minimize taxes, investors may also use tax-efficient investing strategies to help keep more money in their pockets. One of the most important tax-efficient investing strategies is to invest in tax-advantaged accounts such as a 401(k) or the previously discussed IRA> Contributions to these accounts are typically tax-deductible, meaning that you may reduce taxable income by the amount you contribute. These accounts grow tax-free, meaning that no taxes will need to be paid until the money is withdrawn in retirement. By investing in these accounts early as a young investor, you can take advantage of the power of compounding to grow wealth over time while minimizing tax liability.

Another tax-efficient investing strategy is to consider the tax implications of the investments made. For example, investing in stocks that pay qualified dividends can be more tax-efficient than investing in stocks that pay non-qualified dividends. Qualified dividends are taxed at the capital gains rate, which is lower than the income tax rate.

Finally, it is important to consider the impact of taxes on your overall investment strategy. For example, if you're investing in a taxable account, you may want to consider investing in tax-efficient funds or exchange-traded funds (ETFs) that track broad market indexes. These investments have a lower turnover rate and generate fewer taxable events, which can help minimize tax liability. Additionally, if you're investing in individual stocks, you want to consider using tax-loss harvesting to offset capital gains realized by selling stocks with a loss. Tax-loss harvesting is simply using the losses to "cancel out" the taxes that you would have to pay on gains.

Overall, tax-efficient investing strategies are important for young investors looking to build their wealth. Being mindful of the tax implications of selling investments and incorporating tax-efficient investments into investment strategies can reduce tax liability and keep more money in your pocket.

11 ALTERNATIVE INVESTMENTS

Introduction to alternative investments

While investing in stocks has a key connotation with the word "investing", there are many other forms of investing that go beyond stocks, bonds, and mutual funds. This is referred to as alternative investments.

Alternate investments are assets that do not fit into the categories of stocks, bonds, or cash. These include real estate, commodities like gold or oil, collectibles like art or coins, and even cryptocurrencies. These investments have characteristics that make them attractive to investors.

One of the benefits of alternative investments is that they provide diversification to a portfolio. Alternative investments will not always move in the same direction as stocks or bonds, so alternative investments are one of the best ways to reduce a portfolio's risk.

While this is true, alternative investments come with unique risks that investors must be aware of. For example, real estate investments can be affected by changes in the local housing market or economy, and collectibles may not appreciate very much. Some alternative investments may not be regulated as traditional investments as well.

When considering alternative investments, it is important to understand the risks, as they are different from traditional investing risks. You should also be aware that these investments may require a larger initial investment and not be as liquid as traditional investments. Liquidity is how quickly an asset can be sold or bought without affecting its price.

One benefit of alternative investments is their potential for higher returns. For example, real estate can generate rental income in addition to appreciating over time, and metals can provide a hedge against inflation. Cryptocurrencies have experienced significant growth in recent years and have the potential for higher returns.

Alternative investments can be an interesting and lucrative addition to a diversified investment portfolio. However, they should be approached with caution and through understanding the risks.

Examples of alternative investments

Real estate is one of the most popular alternative investments. This can include purchasing rental properties or investing in real estate investment trusts (REITs). Owning rental properties can provide steady income through rent payments and the potential for appreciation in property value over time. REITs, on the other hand, allow investors to pool their money with others to invest in a portfolio of properties managed by professionals.

Another popular alternative investment option is commodities. Commodities are physical goods that can be traded, including gold, oil, and wheat. These can be purchased directly or by investing in mutual funds or ETFs that track commodity prices. These can provide diversification as commodities are fully independent of the stock market.

Collectibles, like art and stamps, can be alternative investment options. These items can appreciate in value over time, particularly if they have historical significance. The downside to collectibles is the level of expertise required to ensure that an item is authentic and will hold value.

Investing in private equity or venture capital can provide opportunities to invest in startups or businesses that are not publicly traded. Private equity funds pool money from investors to purchase and restructure businesses, while venture capital funds invest in early-stage companies with high growth potential. These investments can provide high returns but come with higher risks.

Finally, cryptocurrencies have become a popular investing alternative. Cryptocurrencies, such as Bitcoin and Ethereum, are digital assets that can be traded or held as investments. While the values of crypto can be volatile, they provide unique opportunities.

Alternative investments may have high fees and expenses associated with them. Hedge funds and private equity, for example, often charge management and performance fees that can eat into investment returns.

Alternative investments, as previously mentioned, are less regulated than traditional assets, increasing the risk. Cryptocurrencies, for example, are not backed by the government or financial institutions, and their value is subject to large fluctuations based on market sentiment. Similarly, peer-to-peer lending platforms are not insured by the FDIC, and there is no guarantee that loans will be repaid.

In summary, alternative investments offer benefits and risks that must be considered before investing. While these investments can provide higher returns and diversification benefits, they come with inherent risks like illiquidity, high fees, and lower regulation.

12 SOCIALLY RESPONSIBLE INVESTING (SRI)

What is socially responsible investing (SRI)

Socially responsible investing (SRI) is a form of investing that considers financial return in addition to the environmental, social, and governance (ESG) performance of companies. It is also commonly referred to as sustainable investing or ethical investing. SRI gives investors the ability to align investment decisions with personal values and principles.

Investors who practice SRI often consider factors such as carbon footprint, labor practices, and community impact when making decisions relating to investing. For example, an investor may choose to invest in a renewable energy company rather than a fossil fuel company in order to support environmental sustainability.

With environmental considerations, SRI also takes social factors like human rights and diversity into consideration. For example, an investor may choose to avoid companies with poor policies for diversity or companies that have been implicated in human rights violations.

Lastly, SRI considers the governance practices of companies as factors such as executive compensation and board diversity. Investors may choose to invest in companies with more transparent and accountable governance practices.

There are many different ways that investors can practice SRI. One common approach is to invest in mutual funds or ETFs that are specifically designed to align with certain ESG criteria. Another approach is to engage in shareholder activism, where investors use their ownership stakes in companies to advocate for positive change.

Overall, SRI provides a way for investors to align their investments with their personal values and beliefs. It allows investors to support companies that prioritize sustainability and social responsibility and avoid companies that do not. The practice allows investors to earn financial returns and make a positive impact on the world around them.

How to align your investments with your values

The most impactful aspect of SRI is the personalization of the practice. As an investor, you can align your investments with your own beliefs.

The first step in aligning investments with values is identifying what values you want to look for. What is important to you? Do you care about the environment, social justice, or human rights? Once you understand your values, you can research options that align with these values.

One way to invest in companies that align with your values is to look for SRI options. These are investments that already take environmental, social, and governance into account in addition to financial performance. SRI funds avoid investing in companies that negatively impact the environment or engage in harmful practices.

Another option is to invest in companies that are actively working to make a positive impact in the areas that you deem impart. For example, if you care about the environment, you may invest in a company that is developing sustainable energy solutions.

You may also use your investments to support companies that have a strong track record of ethical business practices. You should look for companies that are transparent about their operations and have a commitment to social responsibility. This information can be found on a company's website, in their annual reports, or independent ratings agencies.

It is important to be aware that investing always carries risks, and there is no guarantee that this will be the most profitable means of investing, but by aligning values, you can feel good about where your money is going.

Potential risks and limitations of SRI

One potential risk of SRI is the lack of standards and definitions. There is no universal definition of what constitutes SRI, and various investors may interpret the concept differently. The lack of clarity can add challenges to investors in knowing if companies are truly sustainable and if their claims match their actions.

An additional limitation of SRI is the potential for lower returns. SRI investors may be limited in investment choices when avoiding companies that do not meet their social responsibility criteria. This can limit the potential returns on investments as profitable companies may not align with investors ' values.

SRI may also be very vulnerable to greenwashing. Greenwashing occurs when companies misrepresent their environmental and social impacts to attract socially responsible investors. For instance, a company may claim to be environmentally friendly by reducing its carbon footprint, but it may contribute to environmental degradation. Greenwashing makes it difficult for investors to identify genuine socially responsible companies.

Finally, SRI may not address the root causes of social and environmental issues. Investors may focus on investing in companies that make positive changes, but this may not address the underlying systemic issues that contribute to social and environmental problems. For example, investing in a company that produces eco-friendly products may not address the root causes of environmental degradation, like overconsumption and waste.

Overall, SRI offers a method of aligning investments with values and making a positive impact, but it is essential to understand the risks and limitations of SRI, including the lack of standards, potential for lower returns, greenwashing, failure to address systemic issues, and complexity. Investors must balance the desire to make a positive impact with the need to invest in companies that will provide them with financial security.

13 ADVANCED STRATEGIES

Options trading and how it works

Options trading is a very complex form of investing. In options trading, investors buy or sell the right to buy or sell stock at a specific time and price. It can be profitable, but it is very risky.

There are two main types of options: call and put options. Call options give the buyer the right to buy a stock at a specific price, and put options give the buyer the right to sell a stock at a specific price. The specific price is referred to as the strike price, and the specific time period during which the option can be used is the expiration date.

When investors buy options, they pay a premium to the seller. The premium is the cost of buying the right to buy or sell the stock. If the investor decides to exercise the option, they pay the strike price to the seller and receive the stock. If the investor decides not to exercise the option, they let it expire and lose the premium.

One of the main advantages of options is that they may be used to limit risk. If an investor owns a stock and worries that it will decline, they can buy a put option to sell the stock at a specific price. Then, if the stock declines, the investor can sell it at the strike price to limit their losses.

Options trading also comes with a high degree of risk. Because options have an expiration date, they can lose value very quickly if the stock does not move in the expected direction. Additionally, options are used for speculative purposes. This can result in losses if the investor does not exercise caution.

Options can be a profitable investment strategy, but they come with a high degree of risk. Always do research, invest what you can afford to lose, and choose a reputable brokerage firm to trade with.

Short selling and how it works

Short selling is a method of making money in the stock market by betting against the success of a company. It involves borrowing shares of a company that the investor thinks will decline in price, selling those shares at the current market price, and buying them back in the future at a lower price to return them to the lender. The profit for the investor lies in the difference between the price at which they sold the shares and where they bought them back.

To illustrate short selling, let's say an investor believes that the stock of Company X is overvalued and will decrease in value. The investor borrows 100 shares of Company X from a broker and sells them at the current price of $50 per share, receiving $5,000. Then, if the stock of Company X does fall, the investor can buy back the shares at a lower price, like $30 per share for a total of $3,000. The investor returns the borrowed shares to the broker and makes $2,000 in profit.

To illustrate the risk, if the stock of Company X rises in value, the investor will have to buy back the shares at a higher price, leading to a loss. For example, if the stock of Company X increases to $70 per share, the investor will have to buy back the shares for $7,000 and lose $2,000.

Short selling is risky as the potential losses are unlimited. When investors buy stock in a company, the maximum loss they can have is the amount of money they invested, but when investors short stocks, the losses can be greater, as there is no limit to how high the stock price can rise.

Short selling is also a bit controversial as it involves betting against the success of a company. Some argue that shorting can harm the company's reputation, which poses a question of ethics.

Shorting, betting against the success of a company, involves borrowing shares of a company, selling them at the current market price, and buying them back at a lower price. Shorting can be risky and controversial, but it can be a great opportunity for profit.

Margin trading and leverage

Margin trading and leverage are two important concepts for trading. Margin trading allows traders to borrow money from a broker to purchase securities. Leverage is the use of borrowed funds to increase the potential return on an investment.

When traders participate in margin trading, they are borrowing money from their broker to purchase stocks or securities. This can be useful for investors who want to increase their purchasing power and profits. However, margin trading comes with a lot of risk.

One risk of margin trading is that it may intensify losses. If the price of the securities being traded drops, the trader must still be responsible for paying back the borrowed funds in addition to interest. This can result in a decrease in capital and potentially a margin call where brokers demand additional funds to cover losses.

Leverage is the use of funds that are borrowed in order to increase the potential return on an investment. If an investor has $1,000 to invest and utilizes leverage to borrow another $1,000, they end up with $2,000 to invest. If the investment increases by 10%, the investor then has $2,200. This results in a 20% return on their initial investment.

It is important to note that both margin trading and leverage are only available through specialized brokerage accounts and require a certain level of expertise. These tools may be hard to acquire, but they can allow for significant profits. These trading types are important concepts that come with both risks and benefits, but are worth considering as an investment strategy.

14 CONCLUSION

The benefits of investing in the stock market

Investing in the stock market is a really smart decision for those looking to build wealth and secure a financial future.

One of the main benefits of the stock market is the potential for returns. Over time, stocks have outperformed other assets like bonds and real estate, pointing to the fact that stocks have the potential to yield higher returns in the future. By investing at a young age, there is more time to take advantage of compound interest and growth.

Investing also allows young investors to obtain a valuable education in finance. Through researching individual stocks, young investors can gain an understanding of how companies and industries operate, which can be valuable in future financial decisions like starting a business or buying a home.

Investing in the stock market provides young investors with a range of benefits that assist in building wealth, gaining valuable knowledge and skills, and setting themselves up for a financial future. While investing carries risk, it can reap significant benefits.

The importance of education and learning

Continued education and learning are crucial for young investors as they allow them to develop critical thinking skills, building a foundation for future career paths.

Investing allows young investors to explore new ideas and perspectives logically and analytically. Additionally, investing builds the necessary skills required for a career and even education.

Continued education and learning allow young investors to build a growth mindset and become lifelong learners, preparing them for their personal and professional lives.

Final thoughts and advice for young investors

Investing at a young age can be a great decision as it allows one to take advantage of compound interest over a longer period of time.

First, you must understand your investment goals and risk tolerance. What do you want to achieve with your investments? How much risk are you willing to take? Are you comfortable with the possibility of losing some money to learn? Answering these questions will help guide your investment decisions.

Secondly, diversification is key. Do not invest all your money into a single stock or asset class, as it increases the risk of loss. You can minimize your risk by spreading your money across assets.

Thirdly, start small and be patient. You do not need a large sum to start investing. Many investment platforms allow you to start with $10 or $20. Remember that investing is for the long term.

Overall, investing at a young age can be a valuable way to build wealth and achieve financial freedom while also learning. By following this book's tips and guidelines, you can understand the steps you are taking in order to minimize risks and maximize potential for growth. Invest wisely, diversify portfolios, and be patient.

Good luck!

www.ingramcontent.com/pod-product-compliance
Lightning Source LLC
Chambersburg PA
CBHW070507220526
45467CB00002B/599